THE LONELIEST WALK: MANAGING THE PAIN OF GRIEF

MARY JO MCCABE

&

DR. BHRETT MCCABE

Authors and Publishers Disclaimer

This book and all related publications were written and produced to provide information and commentary on the subject matter presented. This book does not take the place of any professional psychological counseling or other consultative services. The reader should not construe any professional relationship as a result of purchasing this publication. Should professional services be warranted, competent professional agents and services should be sought.

This book has been published by UNITUS PRESS.

The Psychic and The Doc Radio Program is a production of The Psychic and The Doc Radio Program, LLC. It can be heard on radio stations throughout the Southeast United States on Saturday evenings or online at www.thepsychicandthedoc.com.

Table of Contents

To those walking The Loneliest Walk, to realize that you are never alone……

The Loneliest Walk

Chapter 1:
Facing the Journey Before You

Events in life cannot always be planned. One minute, life is normal. The next moment, "normal" is a living nightmare. Life can change in a minute, a minuscule blip on the lifeline, but such great consequences follow. From that moment, life is defined by a demarcation separating the years before and the experiences thereafter. This life-changing event and circumstance were not what you bargained for from the outset, but it is now what forces you to reevaluate every aspect of who you are.

The following is an example that inspired this book. The names and identifying information have been changed for this and all examples throughout the book.

The Walters were the typical American family until one Friday evening when the phone rang to inform them that their 16-year-old daughter was at a local hospital. The call came from her best friend's sister, who learned there had been an accident and told them they needed to come to the hospital. Mother and father rushed there.

That day began as normally as any day over the previous five or six years. Their daughter Meghan went to school with her friends, quickly saying goodbye as she left the house. She and her mom discussed their plans for the weekend, and the conversation led to stereotypical bickering between a teen and her mother. They did not go to bed angry, but there was tension about their plans and her mother's expectations that Meghan complete all of her work before going out for the weekend. Meghan's father was out of town Tuesday through early Friday afternoon and was briefed on the happenings only when he returned home from business. He suggested any disagreements be settled later because he did not have the time at present to address them.

While Meghan was at school, her mother and father were going through their daily routine. All seemed normal until evening. When school let out Meghan asked if she could go directly to her friend's house to plan for an upcoming school dance. Because she would be home later that night, her mother had no concerns. When much later there was no word from Meghan as to when she planned to come home, her mother called her cell phone. Meghan didn't answer. The call went straight to voicemail.

Two hours later, after much frustration, anger and concern, Meghan's parents received the phone call that changed their lives forever. Meghan and her best friend were on their way home when another car crossed the center line. The collision happened in an instant, but its ripple effect upon Meghan's family was everlasting.

When her parents arrived at the hospital, they were greeted by her best friend's family. They did not have any information on Meghan because the doctors wanted to wait on her family. When the doctors learned Meghan's family had arrived, they met in the family conference room. It was there her family learned the news that dramatically changed their perception of life. Meghan was killed in the accident. Her friend suffered a few broken bones, and the driver of the other car was uninjured. Meghan had no chance. Most of the impact occurred on her side of the car. The doctors led Meghan's parents to her to allow them time to spend together, as a family – one final time.

Their plans for the weekend shifted from dinner Saturday night and a family outing Sunday to calling family, arranging a funeral, and simply trying to survive for the next breath. As friends and their families learned of the accident, they gathered at the hospital. The emotions of Meghan's mother and father ran the spectrum from hysteria to calm and business-like. They had things to do, so many they could not determine what should be next. As night became morning, the gathering of friends and family moved to their house, ushering in relatives who arrived from out of town for a painful reunion. Their lives were now filled with support, but that would soon change.

After friends and family left the house, mother and father were alone. The emotional five days that began with normal mother-daughter activities and ended with a funeral and wake took a toll on the family and community. The outpouring of support was overwhelming, but now, other families were returning to their lives, reminded to kiss their children at night, to tell their loved ones how they felt about them and to be thankful for the miracles in their lives. The impact Meghan's life had on them would last, but not in the way the family thought when they had looked at college admissions and possible academic pursuits. Her family remained alone, buoyed by the memories of a better time and shattered by fear of what lay ahead.

Regardless of how much friends and family may help, Meghan's family is starting a journey borne by so many, yet asked for by no one. What lies before them is their own Loneliest Walk. From that weekend forward, their walk challenges their resolve, setting them on a course branded with the pain and uncertainty of the life before each of us. The Loneliest Walk begins...

The title, "The Loneliest Walk," says it all. Alone and empty without direction, searching for answers and hope. The harder you try, the more alone you feel. Meghan's family is an example, a composite of millions of individuals and families who move along their loneliest walk each day. The pain is immeasurable, the anger often indescribable.

Words simply cannot describe the pain in your heart and the absence in your soul after the loss of a loved one. There are few struggles and pains in life that hurt as badly. The cause of death does not matter. The finality, the certainty, and the loneliness define the suffering you experience. There is no 12-step program, medication, or surgery that eases the pain of grief. It is personal and revealing. It is hell on earth.

Too often, grief becomes a badge of despair worn after the passing of a loved one. Your friends and family do not know how to interact with you. There are no user guides for this type of experience. The common inclination is to want to help but not know what to say. As a result, your friends and family avoid calling, stop checking in on you as frequently, and have their own lives that need their attention, leaving you alone, isolated, and yearning for help. You know your family and friends are there for you if you really need them, but it is still difficult to ask, as you are afraid that you will burden them with your "problems." Both sides know what they want, but each is too concerned to ask for it. This is how isolation becomes entrenched.

Much like with Meghan's family, the life-changing event and its aftermath altered your image in your community. You were no longer the parent, spouse, child, or friend of the person that crossed over; you became the one left behind. You became the one saddled with the unbearable pain of loss. It changes your life, alters your identity and worse, challenges the faith you have in yourself and God, your higher power, or the existence of good on earth. You are alive but not living life anymore.

Why in the hell do you have to suffer from something that is inevitable for each and every one of us?

Why would God allow this?

What is the purpose?

Why me?

We have worked with numerous individuals over the years who have sought our services because of the loss of a loved one. Their presentation is often the same as the families who preceded them – the search for proof of life after death, yearning to know that their loved one is safe and OK. Whether the grief is new or prolonged, the experience is the same. It is front and center in their minds. This search often defines their existence. One of the most important aspects of their life has been ripped out with no regard for their personal feelings. How can this happen?

The loneliness of the experience defines the suffering. While you may feel you have strong social supports, friends and family, the difficulty lies not in those around you but your isolation from life itself. Life changes when grieving begins. What was normal is the past, a time when things were better. The future does not offer hope and salvation; instead, it casts a shadow of the unknown on a world with an important member missing.

When your loneliest walk started, you were unaware of the path that lay before you. The walk is a lifetime built by continuous moments of survival. When you started on this path, you did not choose the start or outcome; instead, the journey chose you. What is the purpose behind this? How can you muster the strength to continue to live when life has been ripped from you?

The Loneliest Walk has begun. It is your objective to continue along this life path. You cannot change the fact that you are on this journey, but you can alter how the walk progresses. Regardless of how long you have been on your walk, the first step starts now.

.

Chapter 2:
The Next Step

The grieving process has been a focus of the medical, psychological, and spiritual communities for decades.   There are books and discussions on the stages of grief from an academic viewpoint, and there are spiritual conferences that examine ways to manage the dying process.   In the late 1960s, a brilliant pioneer in the field of grief, Dr. Elizabeth Kubler-Ross, wrote and published the seminal work on the stages of grief, On Death and Dying.   It is required reading, throughout academic disciplines, for those who wish to understand grief. The core of the book is how individuals progress throughout a variety of stages, including denial, anger, and acceptance.   Her work is academic in nature but has been a lifeline for many on their own personal walk.

While it is routinely acknowledged as a personal experience, few have looked as intimately at the grieving process from the perspective that we will explore it in the following pages: how it impacts those around us, and how to lessen the focus on what you are losing and enhance the belief that there is a purpose and meaning behind what you are experiencing.   It does not lessen the pain, but it can put it into perspective. Education is the key to understanding the pain you feel, and through this wisdom comes perspective.

After the ceremonies and memorials ended, Meghan's family tried to return to some semblance of a normal life. Her father returned to work after three weeks off, and her mother tried to find some degree of normalcy in her life. From the outside, it looked like her father had it better. He had a whole life to return to, a successful career, work objectives to meet, and friends at work that could ease the pain. Her father would show up for work, put on a good image, and crash behind the scenes. He was alone in his suffering, reminded of how he would always call his daughter when she got home from school. That had been his tradition since the day she started kindergarten. Regardless of where he was, he always tried to find time to call and touch base. He has reminded himself, to the point of frustration, that on the day she died, he was flying and unable to call. He could not talk with her, and now he cannot tell her how he feels. On the outside, her father remains stoic and composed. On the inside, he is dying.

The family was more concerned about Meghan's mother. Meghan was an only child, the complete center of attention for her mother. Meghan's mother's friends were the mothers of Meghan's friends. Over the years, as the children's activities and interests changed, so did those of the mothers. From soccer to dance, there was always activity around Meghan and her mom. Now, she sits alone at the end of the day, reminded of what was once her life, what lies before her, and wondering how she can make it to tomorrow. She is struck by her husband's composure through all of this. Her emotions are raw and on display; his are removed and distant.

Meghan's parents become more and more distant from each other. The common bond between them, Meghan, was no longer there. Now, their conversations avoid any mention of Meghan because the pain is too deep to discuss.

Her father's work performance continues to suffer, and her mother's pain continues to worsen. Their loneliest walk led them to a world known by many, littered by the footprints left by those who had been on the walk before them. Each footprint left a story, but there was no explanation of who had been on this walk.

Grief comes in all shapes and sizes. It is most commonly associated with the death of a loved one, but it can also be applied to dramatic changes or loss in any aspect of life. That is not to say that the magnitude of grief is the same; rather, the process of managing the pain of grief can be applied to losing a job, an identity, the ending of a period of life, or the death of a loved one. The Loneliest Walk does not discriminate, as the footprints reveal.

Much like a footprint in the sand, grief leaves an impact, an image for those behind you to see. You can learn a lot from a footprint, and you do not have to be a crime scene analyst to learn from what is lying right in front of you. Looking down and learning forces you to pay attention to details you would normally overlook. Pay attention to the details, because a world of information lies in each step along your loneliest walk.

If you pay attention to the footprints, you can learn if those who walked before you continued walking or if they turned around and gave up. Most importantly, you can learn where the footprints were accompanied by others and when they were alone. Who survived the walk, who persevered, and who rallied to bring others along the journey can be ascertained by simply paying attention to the footprints on the path. Further, these footprints vary in sizes. Some will represent a strong, tall man with deep, pressing foot indentions. The ones before those may represent a diminutive child, walking with a quicker pace but on the path towards the goal in sight. Footprints on the path provide the guidance for you and share a new perspective for you on your loneliest walk. Each is moving forward, regardless of size, depth, or shoe style.

Start looking at grief from a new perspective, as a journey along a path that will lead to a great garden of enlightenment. There may be many thorns along that path, detours to avoid difficulty, and times when giving up seems like a logical decision, but trust that the rewards you seek are not that far away. It is a new perspective.

What do you have to lose?

What can you learn from your own footprint? Take a look back at your progress. Examine whether you allowed someone to walk beside you, or if the footprints show people turning away from you. Learn from the depth of your footprint, because there are times when you are carrying a greater load, and other times when your walk has a better pace. Your emotional load does not have a weight limit.

From the moment you learn your loved one passed away, you are flooded with emotions. It does not matter if you have had the time to prepare for the crossing or if it is sudden, like the result of an accident, because the reactions are very similar. It is a sledge hammer on the cuticles of your fingers, with the pain traveling through each and every aspect of your existence.

How do you manage this pain and still live on?

Along the walk, you have been faced with great challenges, emotionally and spiritually. Birthdays, anniversaries, graduations, and weddings remind you of your loved one. The emotional burden of each recurring event has the potential to further isolate you on your walk. They remind you of what you no longer have, what you are missing from life now, and that these will continue to hurt in the future. They do not cause you to love less; rather, they challenge you to believe that love continues.

Love does not understand the difference between life on earth and life on the other side. You do not stop loving after someone crosses over. Just because they have left the physical realm does not mean that the emotions of love and connectedness no longer exist. These thoughts should not go away. They remain a part of you.

Two birthdays and two Christmas holidays came and went for Meghan's parents. The first year, they chose not to celebrate either. It was too painful. They received a few birthday cards and donations made to a local charity, a few friends dropped by to reminisce, and a few shared stories and pictures. It was therapeutic for her friends but devastating for her family.

When graduation for Meghan's class approached, her parents struggled with the decision to attend. They wanted to support the many families that had supported them, but the reminder that these children that they had known for so many years were moving on with their lives without Meghan was too painful.

After phone calls from the school's principal and counselor, they decided to attend. The senior class created a slide show with photos of their journey through high school and wanted to honor Meghan. The principal and counselor asked if her parents wanted to see it in advance, but they declined because they were not sure if they were going to attend at all. They confirmed their attendance, but dreaded that date as it approached.

Over the past two years, Meghan's parents were faced with many difficult choices. They had independently continued to struggle along their walk. There were time their footprints were together; other times they were apart, one in front of the other. At times, both stood completely still, not moving. This graduation was a time their footprints came to a complete stop--a crossroads in their life, a hurdle in their grieving. Or so they thought.

The greatest fear that they had about the graduation was that by attending and being around the happy families, they would be reminded by how much they missed their daughter. What would she be doing now? Wouldn't she be enjoying this?

With much support from friends and family, Meghan's family attended the graduation ceremony. They were seated in the auditorium with the other families of graduating seniors. Meghan's name was called in line with everyone else, a decision that was approved by the school board but not announced to the family. The auditorium had a moment of silence to honor Meghan and her family. As graduation moved on, the time for the slide show got closer. Her family was very anxious about the unknown, the reminders of what they no longer had, the concern over how Meghan is now, and most importantly, the wondering if she is OK, living and loving on the other side. Their faith says yes, but the doubt always remains.

When the slide show began, the images were filled with laughter and love, reminders of a time when life was easier. While they were emotional, it was a beneficial experience, as they were able to honor Meghan among friends and families that had also grieved and gone along their own loneliest walk. Meghan's parents soon realized that the other footprints on their path were those left behind by their friends and family. There were times when the footprints formed a group, like birthdays, holidays and graduation, and times when they were alone, each feeling isolated at different points along the path.

After the graduation, Meghan's parents and her friends shared time to remember Meghan privately. It was a time for each to remember her, share their thoughts, and voice concerns for Meghan. They wanted to know if her parents were all right and if they thought Meghan was OK. Some expressed angst that they were worried about Meghan, since their faith said that she was in a better place. Meghan's parents united the group, bringing the footprints together and supporting each other along their individual Loneliest Walks.

You are not alone on this walk, although you may feel isolated from life itself. This overwhelmed sensation results from the flood of emotions, the changing of your identity, and uncertainty about the future. This feeling does not go away completely over time. It stays with you. Trust that you are not alone. Life has not left you – just an important part of your life. Not life itself.

You are on The Loneliest Walk – Do Not Walk It Alone. You are never alone. Trust that your life will not abandon you. The life you have lived has been created to guide you and accompany you, not isolate you. You may feel alone, but that will pass. Pay attention to your surroundings, as they will tell the story that you desire.

Look around at the footprints that have walked beside you. They need you as much as you need them. Extend your hand, lend a shoulder, and listen. The world of life after death is opening up to you. Be willing to listen.

Chapter 3:
The Flood of Emotions

Meghan's parents made it through the graduation ceremony and the following months. It was not easy, as the summer was a time for family vacations and gatherings. Meghan's friends prepared for college and their parents prepared to send their children out into the world. Meghan's parents were happy for them, but this time also reminded them of what they had lost – the experiences with Meghan.

Meghan's mother and father continued on their walk, individually. While there were times they relied on each other, for the most part their grieving was an individual experience. Her father, once on the fast track on his corporate ladder, fought hard to remain successful. The endless battles and sacrifices for the sale did not feel as important as they used to. As a result, he was passed over for several promotions and became increasingly frustrated with his work life. What was once a buoy in his own rough waters became a source of emotional turmoil.

Meghan's mother was stuck in a different perspective. Between her own personal struggles and staying busy to maintain an outwardly normal appearance to the rest of the community, her mother struggled with her own thoughts of Meghan and Meghan's welfare. Through parties, family gatherings, and her friends' celebrations, her mother could not escape from the concern and empathy of what Meghan was missing. It was not fair that a child that did everything right would have to miss the bounties life had to offer. She was taken away too early.

These concerns consumed her mother. She could not focus on her own grieving because she could not let Meghan go. Her friends and family became increasingly concerned, offering suggestions to overcome grief, and shared personal stories about their grief. Through each story, the message was that she should have been over her grieving at that point. It was time to move on. How could she move on when she was concerned about Meghan's welfare?

The Walters family continued along their own Loneliest Walk. They were consumed with different emotions but similar in that neither allowed them to work through their own grief. Both were more concerned about the other, concerned about Meghan's welfare, and yearning to know if she was OK. Not only were they on their Loneliest Walk, they were doing so with the emotional backpack of guilt, empathy, and stuffed emotions. The walk was hard enough without adding the weight of things they could not control or impact.

Grief is filled with a variety of emotions. Over time, you will experience a wide range of emotions, process some, and avoid others. There are no systematic ways you go through the emotional experiences, but eventually, you will go through all of them.

One of the most common emotions that can add unwanted emotional baggage to those on the walk is empathy. The concern for the well-being of your loved one should not diminish because they have crossed over. Your empathy and emotional investment do not change simply because they have died. You still want to know they are safe, with loved ones on the other side, that the transition was painless, and that they know you love them.

Your empathy does not diminish after they die. Instead, your emotional concern and empathy intensify because all you have left to remain connected are your worries and concern. When the physical connection is gone, all you have left is the emotional bond. It is completely natural Empathy remains, but it is different.

Were they scared?

Were they in pain?

Do they know the pain I am feeling now?

It is easier to focus on your loved one than yourself. Empathy can become that unwanted baggage when you allow it to rob you of the emotional experience you need. Whether it is guilt over the circumstances of the death or mixed feelings about moving forward in life, this emotional baggage prevents you from progressing on your walk. It keeps you stuck in the moment, a period of time that is miserable and painful.

Anger is similar to empathy and common throughout the grieving process. It can be focused on the loved one who died because they left you behind, expressed because of how they died, or directed at the world at large. The truth remains that anger is only a symptom, not the cause. It taps into the emotional upheaval you experience during the grieving process. However, like empathy, there is a purpose behind anger – motivation.

Over the past several generations, society has rewarded selflessness and discouraged selfishness. In schools and parenting guides, it has been taught that it is important to make sure everyone else is taken care of before you take care of yourself. The fear is that focusing on you is selfish and comes at the expense of everyone else in your life. Interesting philosophy, but wrong.

When you suffer from grief, the emotional toll exhausts your energy and resources available to live life. The empathy for the loved one who crossed over, the struggle to maintain a positive presence for friends and family, and avoidance of emotions each takes a toll physically, emotionally, and spiritually. Becoming consumed with the uncertainty of death and their well-being robs you of your grieving process. This is not to say you are not to have empathy. The difference is to place it behind your own grieving. You are not any good to the world around you unless you care for yourself first. It is hard to believe, but it is true.

In the beginning, it is hard to understand the process and purpose of death and grieving. You cannot simply remove someone from your life, nor would you want to. You still feel for them, concerned that their well-being remains intact. It is a combination of survival and avoidance, all mixed into one. This is why you cannot simply "get over" grief. You move through grief.

Anger, empathy, sadness, and the other emotions you experience during grief do have a purpose. Each serves to move you along the path if you understand them and do not become caught up in their wake. The emotional baggage that accompanies you on your walk does not have to be carried. It can be examined, understood, and processed. That is the learning. It is your learning. Engage it.

It is easy at first to focus on everyone else around you and avoid grieving. You can only deflect grief for so long. Eventually your emotional wall will break, forcing you to deal with the emotions you have fought so long and hard to avoid. It is inevitable.

Meghan's parents kept the world at a distance emotionally. From the outside, they appeared to have it together. They managed to live life each day, saying the right things, so that everyone in their life would check in and give them the encouraging words. It was what everyone wanted. Things appeared good, but they were breaking down.

Meghan's father could not keep up the façade at work and her mother could not keep the emotions at bay for long. It was time to start moving on their loneliest walk, to put down the emotional baggage and start learning from the process. Their individual paths to the crossroad had been different, but the destination was the same. They were not able to avoid the emotions. Much like the graduation ceremony they tried to skip, they could not skip living life. The journey was long, but right. Their walls were ready to crumble, but they needed the push.

On the three-year anniversary of Meghan's death, the crack in the wall occurred. Before, friends and family would call to check in on Meghan's family. They would stop by to talk and reminisce. It was therapeutic for everyone, walking together on that journey. Meghan's parents had been able to go along with the visit and talk and it did relieve some of the emotional pressure in the past. However, this anniversary was different. Only a few called to check in on them. No one came by, not even close family. Meghan's parents were alone, feeling abandoned by life. The past visits had been so helpful, and they appreciated the support. This year was completely different. There was gradual release. It was a complete meltdown, the emotions flooded.

Anger, hopelessness, and despair smothered their existence. Nothing was safe, no one was spared. Meghan's parents' emotional wall crumbled. Her mother and father, for the first time, were forced to take the next step on The Loneliest Walk. The next one was the loneliest and most revealing.

Up to the collapse, Meghan's parents worked so hard to keep it together. They had put on the image others wanted to see. They were angry because Meghan was missing the wonders of life while they were left here to suffer. She was supposed to outlive them, not the other way around. Over the past three years, they learned that others were on this walk, too, but now they learned that this walk required them to take the next step--not for Meghan, not for friends, not for family, but for them. The next step was the most important, as it was about them. The emotional breakdown exposed the essence of who they were and that they were the ones in control of the journey.

It was a moment of clarity. The emotional baggage was put in its place, and they appreciated and respected the other footprints on that path. Those footprints were no longer serving as a guide. They became an example to persevere on this path. When things got difficult, the footprints got deeper but also showed shorter strides. They did not stop. They did not turn around. Most importantly, these footprints revealed there were those who walked beside, walked behind to give a little push, walked in front to pull them along and share the load that they carried. The walk was theirs - no one else's. They had to take the next step for them. They realized they were not alone on The Loneliest Walk, as they were accompanied by the most important person in their life – themselves.

The emotional walls put up during grief can only keep emotions at bay for so long. It is like the dam giving way to the pressures of the flood. Eventually, a crack is exposed, the weakest brick in the wall identified. The flood of emotions follows - the breakdown, the emotional release.

Unfortunately, like any flood, debris is always right behind, floating downstream. The emotional debris is the feelings, concerns, and anger you have been deflecting since the crossing. They never went away; instead, they festered - a weakness in the wall, an emotional experience.

Just like after a flood, when the experts try and determine what went wrong and what was effective, you are left with the desire to understand your own rights and wrongs. It is the progression that now moves to searching and proving that life is there: it continues in you here and in the loved one on the other side. The search is to find the confirmation that your faith has been right all along, in particular, that life does exist after death, alive in spirit, loving you, and knowing you love them. It is as important to you as to them.

Proof of life after death requires listening, learning, and trusting. All three are difficult. Each requires constant reassurance to prevent doubt.

You feel violated, as if someone has broken into your house and robbed you of your most personal items. In fact, they have – your experiences.

There is a process to grief, and there is a process to death. If you are burdened in this life by their crossing, they must deal with it on the other side, too. In living, your emotions and burdens of life impact everyone around you as well.

Think of a time in your life when it became difficult. How did that impact everyone around you? Why is this any different? We are all connected in some form or fashion - emotionally connected, spiritually connected. How do you manage this burden and release your loved one to live?

This is the reason grief is personal. It forces you to examine the meaning behind your emotions. You are forced to relive experiences, good and bad. It is a memory speed dial. As a result, your management of grief is also personal. It progresses on your schedule, on your plan. This is because you set the schedule to deal with these emotions, processing them and the related memories. Take a look at your footprints.

Life is a path of searching. When we stop searching, life becomes lost. We stop living. There is a master plan. You just don't know what it is. The time will come when it all makes sense.

Pain must be dealt with because it is there for a reason. It may be there to force you to deal with the experiences you have been avoiding, to examine who you are or to open up to others. That is the purpose of pain, not asking why they had to die. That is part of the master plan. Grief is not about them, it is about you. When you become so focused on them, you lose focus on the learning for you. You become stuck because you can't move past what you cannot control, what you don't know.

Learning about the process of death and grief frees you to continue to love your loved one. Don't miss the purpose of living and death – your own personal walk. That does not minimize the loved one. In fact, it reinforces their interactions with you, helping develop who YOU are, not what they are. You are the one to live on, to carry on their image, their presence. Do it within your image. That is when you uncover your soul – that nature of you that replenishes those around you.

Why is this important? Knowledge leads to understanding - only then can you grow. Educators have long known the only way to ensure that students were learning was to test them. If you did not have tests, you would not study. Studying leads to learning. I am sure you would say that you would learn, but there would be no urgency, no reason to study.

Should you grieve? Absolutely, because it forces you to uncover the nature of who you are. It is unlikely you would have ever uncovered that aspect of you unless you were forced to. Grieve with understanding, with purpose. Within your faith. Extending your faith. Accept what you are going through because it is with purpose.

Grief is a personal process, one that is managed with each and every step you take. As long as you keep walking forward, focused on the next step, you are progressing. There are no wrong ways as long as you are moving forward, focused on something. Don't stand still, don't sit down, and sure as hell don't give up. There is a purpose to this madness.

You are on the loneliest walk of your life. Working through the pain of grief is a personal journey. It is not fair nor is it right. It is what it is. You cannot go back and change the events that started you on this walk. You now have a choice before you – do you take the next step, or do you give up?

Giving up is not an option. It is never an option, even though you may want to. You would not have made it this far if you were ready to turn back. Take the next step toward moving through the pain of grief. Take the next step on your Loneliest Walk by learning, listening, and experiencing the emotions that you have felt for so long. They are a part of you, get to know them.

The remaining chapters in this book are for those ready to take the next step on their personal journey. Each chapter contains teachings relevant to the grieving process from Mary Jo McCabe and The Guides. The teachings are relatively unedited, as pure to the original message as possible. It is important that you interpret the messages as to what they mean to you. You will find the teachings enlightening and educational.

Chapter 4:
Grief

In this teaching, The Guides encourage us to grieve for those we have lost, but we must not grieve to the point that we stop living our life here on earth. Many of my clients have lost children. How do you tell someone not to grieve too long for their child? You don't. Just as The Guides teach...grief is a personal journey. Everyone grieves in their own way, regardless of the support they have around them. For me to tell them that their child is happy and well gives them little comfort when their heart is so broken. They have to grieve in their own way. And if that grief begins to steal their life, then it is time for their support system to step in and prop them up. That is when they must start the journey of true healing.

I found this teaching to be one that touched my heart. I hope it touches yours as well. Feed off of The Guides' words. They are filled with support and unconditional love. You are truly blessed with their devotion in helping you heal your heart.

--Mary Jo

A Teaching from The Guides:

When someone leaves your world, you feel as though it has not happened. Even though you acknowledge the loss, it does not feel real. At first your focus is only on the person you lost. You may spend days, weeks, months, and years focusing on them – the loss of them. You mourn them. You think of them as they were. You think of them as a ghost in your life. You mourn their youth. You mourn what they will miss in not living their life. You communicate with them in all ways and you even think you see them at times. Your grief is only for them and the life they lost. Even if your loss is someone older in years, you feel there is still a part of life that they will miss, regardless of their age. You do not yet acknowledge that the world in which they live is no longer confined by walls and limitations.

Yes, when you first experience the loss of someone, you feel for them. You worry about them. The thoughts and feelings you have take time to soften. But there are many who never move past this stage of loss. It is the way they distract themselves from grieving their loss. They feel that as long as they search and connect to them with their grief, they create a secure place for them in their life.

While that can be healing, it can become unhealthy if it consumes their life. When they allow every part of their life to be consumed looking for them or searching to connect to them, they take from themselves their own life. More importantly, they rob the person who died from creating and living their new life.

In the world in which we live, we understand that in the first stages of your grief, you are consumed by the concern for the one you lost. We see the sorrow in you, as do they. They see the need for you to connect to them. They feel the pain you carry in your heart. You think of their hardships, the fear they perhaps felt when they died, or who met them when they crossed over. Your entire life is about them – wondering where they are – wondering what they are doing – thinking of what they see in their world. What do they do with their time? Do they eat? Do they feel? Do they see you? All of your thoughts are focused on them. Your grief is for them and that is truth.

During these difficult periods they try hard to help you communicate with them. They want you to know that they are indeed awake, alive, and hopeful. They are truly recreating themselves. They are rejuvenating and creating new interest. Yes, they grieve your loss for them. Yes, they grieve losing you. But to them it is only a short time before they will reconnect to you.

So, you see it is truth that souls that enter into the spiritual world feel the burden of those they have left. They find themselves wanting to comfort and console. Many times this takes from them the existence of their new world. It takes from them a life that must be ignited.

But there is no time that is right or wrong to grieve or no particular path that is the most effective. In the beginning, all grief is consuming. You cannot imagine your life without them. Therefore, you wonder about their new life. You spend much of your time in search of understanding their new world. You find ways to study and to broaden your own spirituality, your own connection to God. You start the journey of seeking to understand the whys. You might even question what the lesson of death is, or what the lesson is of any loss you might have. Thankfully, that is when you begin to look for ways to escape the feelings that you are feeling, that you are having. You just want these painful feelings to disappear.

This is just the beginning in healing, when you begin to search, looking for answers, working to understand what is beyond life. You acquire knowledge that will continually deepen your desire to connect to your wisdom. And when you connect to your wisdom, you find a new life of understanding. You learn that death is as much a part of living as breathing is. You realize that in order to live, you have to die. You realize that in order to die, you have to live. It all fits together like a puzzle in God's world.

It is truth that in your world, if there is pain you cannot ignore it. It will continue to gnaw at you until you are forced to confront it. The pain of loss will continue to chew on you, to gnaw on you until you fully confront it, understand it, and begin to heal it. And the beginning step in healing your pain is to learn to reconnect to your soul, to touch the God part of you. Until you are able to do that, you are focusing only on the person that is lost. The death is still all about them, and not about you.

We want you to know, though, that there is no mystery to death. With everything that happens in life there is a give and a take. You are in a position of loss, and from it you will gain. Perhaps you are afraid that if you accept the loss, if you focus on the lesson for you, it minimizes the person who has gone through the death. In actuality, it empowers them, for they see the purpose of the loss for you in experiencing the loss. They also know that if you are unable to connect spiritually, you will continue to stay in only what has been taken from you. Therefore, they try to help you shift into your higher mind to understand the gift.

It is then that you begin to uncover that part of you that is soul. There you discover the link between life and death. Suddenly you gain a new understanding of the reason, the purpose of the loss. Knowing the reason and purpose for the loss will bring forth knowledge that will uncover your inner wisdom. As you acquire this new knowledge, you will slowly sink into your wisdom. From there, you will bring forth understanding. From there, you will bring connection to the spiritual world. That, my dear ones, is when you begin to confront the anger and depression from the loss. You find you no longer need to label your emotions. You are free to have them and you can recognize that the soul that has been lost is in a better place. You cannot save them from wherever they are. You can only pray for them, connect to them through memory, but now you must save you. That is the responsibility you have in all losses in your life.

And so it is important that you begin the process of healing you, for you no longer have the authority or the know-how to heal the soul that was once a part of your life. You begin the process of taking care of you. You reach out to those around you that have endured such a loss as you. You begin to communicate your feelings to those you trust. You begin to plan for life, creating a different life. You are aware that life will never be the same, so you start to look for new life. Accept that as long as you are alive, you have a message to tell. You have not lost your physical life. You have just lost a part of it. You are left here to live out your message. To begin healing from the loss you have experienced, it is important that you acknowledge, accept, and understand your loss. Until you do, you will be lost in grief. Face your anger. Embrace your sadness. Accept your depression. Tell your story to others. Express yourself through words in whatever way you can, for it unwraps the gift of the loss. And for that it is truth.

Good day.

Chapter 5:
Putting Death in Its Place

Many of us are taught that death is a punishment of some kind. In actuality, that is the farthest thing from the truth. Any death that is experienced is well earned. Somewhere in our walk through life, we learned what we needed to learn on a soul level. Also, if you study the teachings of The Guides, they teach that no one dies accidentally. Every death, every loss is calculated right down to the last breath, even the deaths that scream "accident."

So how do you as a human being find comfort when you are forced to face death? You find *your* way to Putting Death in Its Place. You read. You listen. You share. The more you read about loss, the more understanding you will have concerning death. That certainly doesn't mean you fully embrace it, but you have more peace about it.

You listen. You listen to every person who has their story to tell. From them you will learn how they walk The Loneliest Walk. After all, there is no instruction manual for this walk. Everyone's walk is personal.

You share. You have a story to tell that needs to be heard, so talk. Through your words and efforts, you will teach those who are experiencing or will go through loss while on this earth journey. No one, and I mean no one, will ever escape death. Each and every person will step into that experience.

Read this lesson slowly. As you read, pretend you can hear the words spoken. It will not only benefit you and your healing process, but it will help heal others as you find more peace in your loss.

--Mary Jo

A Teaching from The Guides:

Souls look at death in many ways, some positive and some negative. If they can see death as a welcoming of life, it helps them to put death in the right perspective. Unfortunately, death often creates hardships for those who are left behind. It leaves an empty space.

After souls make their transition to the other side, they are given an explanation as to the reasons for their death at that particular time. It is a way of satisfying that intense desire souls have to know why their journey on earth was taken from them. It matters not how old they were or how young they were when they left the earth path; they are shown why their life was complete. They are given an idea of where they were on their journey as a spiritual being, not as an earthly being. They are shown areas that they came to earth to achieve long before they set foot on earth. At the same time, they are given a clearly defined record of what they accomplished while living life.

Too often death becomes a paralyzing force when you do not view yourself as being eternal. It causes you to fear death itself and often it causes you to fear living life. We understand your fears, but death is really a blessing. It is not a hindrance; it is a beacon of light that allows you to see the true purpose of your life on earth.

When you enter into our world, you are reminded of all you have gained in strengths as well as what you have gained in weaknesses. In fact, you are shown your weaknesses even before you are shown your gains so that you can recognize the measure of your value while on earth. Then when you look at the areas of your strengths, you can see the pattern of your life as you lived it. When you look at areas that were not strong, you can see the reasons you were put in those particular life situations.

As you go through the patterns that were not as successful as you would like, you can see the courage it took for you to embrace them or even attempt them. You are given ideas why your world became so jumbled up, and you are shown what caused the problems that pushed you off your path. During your life, you had difficulty in seeing the reasons behind the struggles you were going through. It is not until you die that you can look at them in an honest way and see the effort it took for you to deal with them.

When you die, you are handled gently. You are taken from the earthly life and very quickly nudged into a place that is warm and secure. You are given opportunities as well as authority, and you are able to speak your own choices and needs. You are given a measure of conversation and shown the principles of "your" truth, and you are given insight concerning what you have accomplished while on earth.

Death is truly a time of reunion. Many are there to not only applaud you for the efforts you made while living life, but they are there to support you in making your transition. You are never shamed or criticized for your earth journey. There is no one to hit you on the hand or scold you in any way. Once on the other side, you are able to understand yourself better, and that alone offers a wonderful healing for you. You are released from the pressures you experienced on earth, and you are made aware of what death really is – freedom. When you see death in this way, you begin to relax and sense the fullness and sincerity of life -- a time which can take one day, one hour, or even years. You are never rushed through the process.

You will be met by those you knew while here on earth, but not always those who were your friends or family. They are in their own space. Many of your soul companions here are much more connected to you than your children, your parents or your friends could ever be while on earth. Because of that, you are much more connected to those who serve and honor you spiritually than those you knew for a short time on earth.

That does not mean those you knew on earth do not join hands with you or have you in their thoughts. It does not mean they do not embrace you. They honor you. When you do see them, they bring you a blessing of love that encourages you to feel comfortable in your new surroundings.

As you make this progression, you begin to move into those areas that allow you to truly see your journey, what you have accomplished, and who and what have pushed you forward in your evolution. You move into the angelic realm – into the fullness of light and the hope and duration of your own eternal plan.

Once entering the spiritual world, you begin to understand the power of those who truly touched your lives and helped you gain momentum while living an earthly life. If you have concern as to why you died in the manner you did, you are quietly reminded that you choose to die in certain ways to experience the lessons you have not learned.

For instance, if your body is diseased when you enter our world, you are wilted. Through the disease that has damaged your body, you have lost a great deal of your strength. You are not anxious or afraid, but you need time to restore yourself. You begin to look for the resources that will help you do this soon after you enter our world. You are also given cushions of light and are brought into a place of healing, where you are given the attention you need. This attention helps you heal and restore your spirit.

It takes time to heal, to bring back to life the part of you that died, the part that dried up and withered while working your life. That is why you come into our world wilted, but not without hope and courage and peace in your heart.

Those of you living life should bless those with your prayers who die in great pain and help them to find their way through their healing process. That doesn't mean there is pain here. There is not, but it takes time for souls to recover from the loss of life they endured on earth.

An example of this is when you have a major obstacle in your physical health. You concentrate on healing you and getting stronger each and every day. It is the same here. It is just done on a deeper level. The pain of life and death is felt from a much deeper place.

The soul who enters into our world wilted from a diseased life is given nourishment that will begin to fertilize and feed his spirit. Then the soul automatically begins to feel a new purpose to live once again.

Another death you question is accidental death. If you leave the earth accidentally, you come into our world fully awake. And while it is hard for those who are left behind, it is not so hard for the souls making the transition to the other side. There is no illness, no diseases in their mind, and they come into our world in full bloom. They have a great spirit about them which makes some of them feisty. They constantly want to prove to themselves that they are dead, especially if they have no knowledge of life after death. Even those who do have knowledge of life after death are often not aware of their death at first. It takes some time for them to fully awaken to where they are.

After adjusting to their new life, they enjoy carrying on conversations with those already here. It is as if they are trying to catch up on lost time. They are given opportunities to explore where they are and what they can become. They are in a place even greater than the best place in your world. And the wonderful part about it is that all souls will spend eternity there – no dread, no pain, no disruption. Souls bask in the joy of that wholesomeness in this heavenly place.

Death from suicide is concerning to all. While that is of great distress to you, to us it is no different than any other death. We see it as a disease. Mental illness affects the emotions and destroys the body physically as well as mentally. Suicide is a choice that is made, even if it is made reluctantly, but to the soul who chooses to die in this way, it feels like an escape.

Think about your own life and the pace of life you keep. Too often you rush through your life, never taking the time to truly enjoy it. Many times you are not even aware of what you have encountered or what you have learned because of the pace you keep.

Not everyone is able to handle the pressures of life, with its constant spontaneity and rush. Those in the physical recognize that the person who commits suicide places an imprint or logo upon them. But we ask you to think about how you treat yourself. When you are not blessing you and treating you fairly or giving to you completely, then you are starving you. You become small in your thoughts, and you die a slow death simply because you do not care for yourself in the way that you should.

When you know you are harming a part of you, it is a slow death. So please don't point your finger in the face of someone who needs help. Instead, reach out to them. Make an attempt to help them. Ask questions and listen. Become interested in them. Your efforts might be that one thing that could change that person's world.

Death also comes to those who become addicted to various things. As you are aware, there are many causes of addictions and many kinds of addictions. Some of you are addicted to work or even food. Some of you are addicted to chemicals or to the patterns of life you keep, especially if you feel denied without it. As strange as it may seem, some of you are addicted to each other. You fear aloneness.

When souls come into our world with addictions, it is hard for them. Usually they are not aware of the multitude of their addictions. They do not realize that even minor addictions can be destructive. Slowly they withdraw from anything that has become a pattern or a habit. They learn that it no longer feeds them. Just as a mother weans her baby from her breast, they, too, must be weaned. That is the way that addictions are dealt with in our world.

As we complete this lesson on death, we ask that you think about death this way. For many, many years you have stood on a high cliff, looking into the valley below. As you look out over the cliff, you wonder if you will ever have the courage to jump. You know that one day someone will join you on the cliff and tell you that it is now your time to jump. You jump.

Death is when you have the courage to jump. When you are free to make that jump, you are taken into a spiral of light, a funnel of light. The moment you jump, you are held up so that the fall is a bounce, not a disaster. You feel as if you are free-falling – the sensation of death. There will be absolutely no fear, no feelings of suffocation. It will be as though you jumped off a high cliff. You have stood so long on the cliff - so long you have waited for the instructions to jump. When it's your time and you are given permission to jump, we encourage you to jump with a sense of peace – not with a sense of dread.

Good day.

Chapter 6:
How We Die

I love this teaching. The Guides take us through the journey of death. Even though they cannot give us the entire story, they have given us great insight into the process of our upcoming transition into the spiritual world. Even though none of us want to learn about death too soon, this teaching offers information I feel we need to know. Read it slowly and savor every word. You never know when you might find this information helpful.

--Mary Jo

A Teaching from The Guides:

As you move into the altar of light, you feel a softness in which you recognize. As you move through this softness, you become a part of it. You lose sight of the physical instantly.

You must realize that upon this earth you choose in life the direction in which you must follow. It is so in that of the spiritual as well. The world in which you know physically has many limitations which you place upon it. In the spiritual, you are given greater freedom, but you are still based in the ideas which you know as your soul. The form in which you take is different than what you take in the physical. In the spiritual, your soul has no form that is physical. It has only a fragrance, and that fragrance creates for you the spark of light that makes you whole.

As you move into the spiritual world, you are led into an altar of light. You are soothed, refreshed, and given nourishment. The nourishment is not of the same rice, the same bean which you serve yourself today. But the substance of which you are given is acceptance, honor, and unconditional love. As you learn how to eat from this source, you find strengthening. This strengthening takes place within the first few hours of your death. You are then made aware of the steps in which you must follow. You are given choices, but you do not always listen to the beings of light there to help guide you. When you do not listen to the elders of the universe, you are unable to connect to the afterlife of yourself. You then are pulled back into the physical and you come into a rhythm of life in which you lose your way.

However, the soul that leaves earth and finds that he is able to hold to the hands of those who have sought to help him begins to open mentally. As he begins to open his thoughts, he begins to find and feel the light.

You see, it is ever so needed that you live within your heart and that you understand the mental capacities of you. It is the mental world that will guide you into the light, not the emotional. So know that the power of thought is the path in which you must follow.

When souls come back into the spiritual world, they will have fear, for there will be an essence of energy which they will feel to be a bit disruptive. Many souls immediately feel panicked. They are unfamiliar with what it is that they see. They feel as though the earth is no longer home and they even become fearful of looking back into that part of them. This sometimes brings them into a stage that makes them linger. They are afraid to move forward; they are afraid to move backward, and so they live in a vacuum. In this vacuum, they can create anything they want; because it is there that they will learn the power of thought if they have not learned it from the physical existence.

Listen to our words well because we are giving to you a map you can follow. You can **find** your path by the way in which you believe, but you can **know** your path by the way in which you think. When you die, it takes both essences in order to build the completeness of what you seek as a soul. If you do not have both essences, you create for you the lingering of what you call earthbound.

Souls that are earthbound are in no way evil. They are in no way destructive, but they are fearful. Because of that fear, they hold themselves in bondage, unable to move into the world of new life, and unable to wean from the path in which they lived.

This is not an unhappy existence by any means. It is a comfortable existence, an existence that many of you know in your physical earth, because it is the same as you would call "just existing."

Let us explain. The routines and the patterns that many of you live your life by, without challenging yourself, without seeking knowledge, lead you to become leveled in the routine you know as your earth life. You are born; you are schooled; you live; and then you die. You do not waste time, but you do not create more time.

When you finally begin to experience the need for more life in your world, you then must make choices as to what that life becomes. If you are given a choice from your higher guidance to live your life longer, it is then you are given a measure to guide you forward into other passages of life. If you have learned what you needed to learn in this life, you then are given the choice to leave this life.

Many of you are taken abruptly, but many of you are taken slowly. For those of you who are taken abruptly, it is the easiest form of death, for your life is lived fully until the day you die. You do not have the fear of death to work through. When you do die, you are truly held in a new essence. It does not say that it is all in this capacity, but it is in most. You are eager to reach for guidance and look for the light.

Many of you, after being fed with honor, love and affection, choose to stay close to the physical. You are not yet ready to disconnect from your family and friends. This does not mean that you are earthbound. It only means that you wean yourself slowly from life.

For the souls who live long and who suffer much, when the final cord has been cut, they feel an instant sense of relief. A chill runs through their spirit, giving to them an instant transfusion of unconditional love. Their spirit is low; their energies are low. It is in this existence that no choice is made. They are held, loved, and healed and never rushed. These souls rock back and forth from the spiritual to the physical. They are given the gift of new life. They are made to feel secure in their new world. They are handled cautiously and carefully. Their teachers seek to bring grace back into their spirit, for their grace has been weakened and they have lost themselves in the pain of their death.

Pain can be degrading to the soul. It humbles the soul. Any time there is pain in the soul, there is pain in the body. Any time there is pain in the body, the soul hurts, too.

Souls that have suffered with much pain may spend lifetimes healing the disease of pain. Miraculously, they are never rushed to heal. They are never forced to make choices. They may leave the earth fully awake even though the spirit of their soul has been damaged in illness and their energy is low. They adapt to their new world very quickly, but it is never short in earth terms. Souls can take many earth years to heal the illness in which they created, but they can also take earth seconds or minutes to heal.

The soul that is mentally awake, that is mentally aware, starts the healing process long before their life ends. As they accept their death and place themselves in anticipation of the transition, the healing process begins. They find hope in eternal life.

As they begin to repair the damage, they are given time. They work softly. They are not kept in silence. They are held in light. They can choose to move around as freely as they wish. They can choose to confront themselves with their counsel as they seek. Many souls wait lifetimes before they ever face themselves in this capacity, but many confront themselves immediately. No soul is brought to the altar without first making the choice to do so themselves.

The souls that end life by their own hand are overwhelmed with sorrow immediately. The pain in which they have removes them from all reality. They know not who they are. They scorn themselves. They want to hurt themselves. These are the souls the angels steal. These are the souls that are given to the world of guardians, to the angels to soothe them, to bring harmony and peace back into their spirit.

These souls heal quickly because of the intensity of the love that is shared with them. It does not mean their passage is easy.

Their passage is most difficult, for the torment of which they have endured comes with them. When they leave the earth in such pain, their soul pushes them into the light immediately. Instead of moving up to the light, they move down in through the light. They approach it from a different capacity. It is harder for them to see the light because of the emotional drowning they have suffered. Their love for themselves has been lost and they are not searching for anything of pleasure, of joy within their spirit.

As souls become awakened in the spiritual, as they begin their process of growth, they still must make many choices. The choices are given to them gently. They are able to be wherever they need to be. Once they leave the physical, they realize they are free. They soar. They no longer need legs on which to walk. All they need is a desire and a thought that can put them anywhere. They are free.

You see our world, the spiritual, is different than yours, the physical. We have gone beyond the physical confinements of life. We work together as one. To us, it is important for you to know that you do have another existence beyond the physical earth and that you must first heal the physical before you are taken back to the home from which you came. It does not mean that you are kept away from your eternal home. It only means that you do not have the desire to go until you finish what you have begun, what you must complete on earth. On a soul level, you understand that truth. It is inbred in your spirit.

But it is not truth that our world is without struggle. Many souls in this spiritual reality have confinements they place upon themselves. This is damaging to the spirit when they are unable to move freely. That perhaps is the closest to what they would call struggle.

As you begin to heal yourself physically, you lift yourself spiritually. Your heart opens. What you are holding as confinement in your spirit, you gently move through. Your thinking becomes broader. Immediately you are shown the light. You make choices quickly. You hear voices, voices which are in many tongues, but you will recognize them, for they are voices of you from long ago.

You see, your death is no different than a birth being given in your earth. There is someone there to catch you. There is someone there to cleanse you. There is someone there that feeds you. There is someone there that clothes you. There is someone there to hand you to your mother. It is the same in our world. There is no difference.

The mother you are given in the spiritual world is the angel of your spirit, your guardian angel, the mother of your soul. From there she will help you make the choices you need to make. You will listen to her words of advice. You will be given control to deliver yourself in whatever capacity you want. You will never be turned away. You will always be accepted. The difference in life in the spiritual and life in the physical is that you cannot die. That is not a choice that is made.

So, my dear ones, life is lived here in great expansion. If you love the mountains, you become a mountain. If you love the sea, you become the sea. If you love the sky, you become the sky. If you are drawn to a color, you become the color. If you like another, you become them. Every feeling, every knowing, and all awareness will become you in whatever way you desire. Life opens for you in broader ways.

Please listen to these words carefully. For those in the physical who have lost those to death, know they are close. Know they have their own life now. Never forget them, but learn to accept where they are. If you hold anger for the loss in which they gave, you will understand it as you begin to mature in their death. Do not make others feel helpless by isolating yourself from your grief. Share yourself openly with those who come to soothe you. You do not have to be alone.

Know that when souls are called back to the earth to serve mankind, they come with joy. There are many who come to your world that are not heard or seen, but they come with love, understanding, and warmth. They serve as mentors for all.

It is not truth that when you leave the earth you lose your arms and your legs, but you do lose a part of you, the ability to touch those that are left. Even if a soul came to you today who has departed from your world, and stood before you, and even if they look solid to you, you would have difficulty feeling their touch. Not because they would not want you to touch them, but they are not of the earth.

So the feeling of touch in which you have today in your world, use it beautifully. It is a gift of earth in which you have. Know that when you touch the hand of another, you give to them a part of you, a part of you that you will never be able to share again: the touch of you. Feel the blessing of the earthly gift of touch.

The death of your soul will never be. The death of your spirit will never be. The death of the physical will indeed come. This is truth.

Good day.

Chapter 7:
You Are Never Lost

Please take time to read this teaching thoroughly. The Guides speak about the darkness, the fear, that we immediately feel when we crossover. What is amazing is they say that we are able to see the light coming from the spiritual realm, but we are unable to see the light or energy from the earth. This must happen when we are being pulled toward the light. In earlier teachings, The Guides have said that the light is like a magnet, one that pulls so strongly that we cannot possibly stop the rushing force that pulls us toward the light. In my heart I know that what The Guides call darkness is just fear on our part, not having the power to change what is happening.

After you read this lesson, ask yourself what you think the darkness means. Remember, there is always an overwhelming, unconditional, embracing love waiting for you when you take your last breath here on earth. I know because I have felt that unconditional love when I met The Guides for the first time. You have never felt anything like what will be waiting for you someday.

--Mary Jo

A Teaching from The Guides:

Death is a mystery. It is a part of life that is as important as being given physical life. There are many ways in which you face death. It does not have to be from dying a physical death. For instance, it can be from the changes in your environment, or the death of a relationship. To know the true impact of death, you need to understand what it brings to you, not what it takes from you.

Allow us to explain. You are born into this life to be able to live your life completely, even though in your mindfulness, you are always aware that one day the end of your physical life will come. If you live fearful of losing your life, this can push you toward an early death. It is not that your attitude must shift, but it is that you must acknowledge your thoughts concerning death.

When souls confront their death, they are forced to let go of the patterns of their past. They may leave the earth path, but that does not mean that the journey of earth is complete for them. It only means that the time in which they existed in this lifetime shifts. In actuality, there is no soul upon earth that exists in life patterns only once. There are many lives that are lived to express the true nature of what the soul needs.

When souls first close their eyes in death, they are embraced in light from the spirit world, but the light of the earth is shut off from the soul who is making the transition. There is a moment of darkness. Call it fear. Call it doubt. Call it anything you like, but around the darkness, there is concern from here for those who are crossing. That moment of darkness is what souls are fearful of, because they fear the confinement of the not-knowing. That truly gives to them much burden while on earth.

In order to confront and overcome your fear of death, you must educate yourself about it. Death is only a shifting of awareness, for the world that you have left must be filtered and must be cleansed from you so that you are free to live and exist in another reality.

You must trust that the moment of death is nothing but a moment. It can seem forever if you are in a place of fear, but know that you are not left there alone. The presence of others that are with you will connect you to the bright light and allow you to see the world that you have entered - not stumbling about but truly feeling the presence of oneness.

When death happens, there is mercy shown to the soul that has crossed. There is no devastation. There is no guilt. There is no burden that is shown to the soul. If there is a burden felt, it is because the soul that is crossing over creates it.

As the soul transitions through death, it is encouraged to take responsibility for the lessons sought and the lessons learned. This enables the soul to discover the truth of what it worked through and owned while living in life. This can be a very fulfilling and joyful experience for the soul and its higher guidance.

We want you to realize that there are many things you can do to prepare for your death. We understand that it is hard for you to know that while in living life, you must prepare for your death. But the only way you will find comfort in death is to become more familiar with the transition.

In order to be more accepting of your death, you must first prepare for the longing that you have been sent to create. Know that you have to plan the journey into death with awareness and with acceptance. It is your duty to work hard to find acceptance in death. More than likely, you will find discomfort and dissatisfaction with the journey until you accept that dissatisfaction, and you are able to distance yourself from it.

Secondly, no matter how lifeless death may seem to you, there is an intensity about it that draws you into its presence. Even though you may see the darkness in death, there is a brightness that shines from it. Remember this truth.

Thirdly, try to be ready for the event of death. This will help those you leave behind as well as those you will meet after your transition. Review the events in your life that you are most proud. Remind yourself of every crisis that you have overcome, every hurt you have healed, and every burden you have eased. Be aware of the hard emotional events in your life, as well. Be aware of the pleasurable events that you feel you have gained in the physical life. Have them foremost in your thoughts. They are yours to keep. They are a part of who you are. But more importantly, they have become what you are. These memories are eternal.

After you leave your earth, you can truly allow your loved ones to experience the joys as well as the sadness in which you felt while still on earth. The gift you leave them is not only your heartfelt moments, but the spirit in you that is eternal.

Good day.

Chapter 8:
The Transition Process

The Guides have spoken on death numerous times, but this teaching is a favorite. Before understanding how to manage the pain of grief, it is important to appreciate the process of death, the miracle of life, and the relationship of both. The Guides describe the spiritual world in a manner that is very familiar to how they speak during readings. It is a community of support, learning, and wisdom.

Your walk on this earth during grief may feel lonely, but on the other side, your loved one's experience could not be any more different than yours. That is reassuring. To understand how to manage the pain of grief, it is important to understand the death process to remove the fear and doubt that accompanies you on the loneliest walk.

--Mary Jo

A Teaching from The Guides:

Death is a structure that a soul experiences. It is as solid and real as life is. Many become fearful of death simply because they do not understand the transition to a different reality. Those from this side do not see death as a struggle. They see death as a choice. Before you came into life, you made choices about how you would enter and how you would leave this earth.

When you face your death, you are brought to mind of all the struggles in time in which you have placed yourself. At first you feel awkward in that emotion and become confused as to which part of you must step away from life. You remember things from your past that you want to take with you. Memories come to you that perhaps you have long forgotten. All of this is done in seconds, as you would time it. You do not have to search deep within you to remember these moments of your past. They are all there, flooding you to help you feel secure in your new world.

It is truth that when you first come into the spiritual world, you enter with an absence of thought. But it does not take long before you begin to resurrect and find the spark of your soul that has grown dim while covering itself with the physical body. As the light of the day is brought forward, as the encouragements are given from your spiritual family and friends, your soul begins to bloom and finds its way into a new life.

It is hard for you to understand the concept of time once you leave your earth. But if I were to give to you a lesson of learning about death, I would teach you this one thing. Be humble in your heart in facing death and know that no matter what takes place in your life, it is not as though you have struggled for nothing to live your life. You have given yourself a blessing for having lived life. Even though you may come into your life innocent, you do not leave your world innocent. You come here with many of the packages that you have worked so hard to wrap, the treasures that you believe have been given to you as your gifts. More importantly, the ones that you will value most are the gifts you gave away to those you loved and cared for while on earth.

While living your life, you are aware that your transition of death is always in front of you. It is not something you can keep from happening. But your life will not end before you fulfill the journey of truth which you need to have as a spiritual being while here on earth. Perhaps the most important thing for your soul is that you pay the debt that you hoped to clear before coming into this life. Once the debt is paid for the physical, the sheet is balanced, and you are free to live new again in the world of angels.

If you live committed to living a Godly life, you will have no difficulty in transitioning into the other world. Those of this world will be focused on helping you be more aware of you and your strengths. They will be encouraging you not to look at what you would see your weaknesses to be, but motivating you to see all the strengths in you.

You may become frustrated when you discover that the road from the physical to the spiritual is not made clear. You have to understand that it takes effort to fully enter into the cave of man, the physical, but it also takes effort to leave the cave of man. Perhaps you may feel as though the last breath draws you into the light of the spiritual world. That is truth. But it is much more complex than that. The joys of living new again in the spiritual realm are simply dimmed somewhat by the grief of leaving behind those who are in pain.

So we say to you that the greatest gift you can give to those who have crossed over is the joy you feel for them for making this transition and to look for the messages they send you. If you ignore the messages given, you will soon receive no messages. You must acknowledge each message as a truth that is real – for it is so. It is important, however, that you acknowledge your feelings of heartache, but you must also acknowledge their feelings of inner peace. For that is truly what they have among them and what they hope to keep around them.

The joy of living is an expression of truth that you seek from the day you are born until you leave the earth. The joy of living here in our world is given automatically, for the warmth of truth that you lived penetrates you like a spark of energy that has given life to the fire that has burned out. We encourage you to feel the treasures that this truth offers you.

Lastly, look for the passages. Look for the transitions in all of life. There is no map to follow. This is your personal journey to live through the transition of life and the transition of death. Your journey is unique and brings to you the wellness that your soul so needs. Unfortunately, you may not realize the blessing of life until it is your appointed moment to let go of it.

Good day.

Chapter 9:
Confronting Death

After reading this lesson, you will know how important it is to connect to each other. The Guides remind you how helpful it is to pray for those who have crossed over into their world. Every time you pray for someone on the other side, they feel your love for them. Can you imagine how great that is for the soul who is lucky enough to receive your heartfelt prayers? To me, it would be the same as winning the lottery. What a gift!!

--Mary Jo

A Teaching from The Guides:

If you stray from the path of your life, you feel dead in the realities in which you walk. It is always through the study of your thoughts that you explore your life emotionally. It is through your emotions that you learn to conquer the self in you that feels dead. This is the beginning path of you confronting the journey into death.

There are various deaths in your world. It does not always mean that you must draw your last breath in order to experience death in life. You become dead in your emotions when your soul has been blistered, or when you feel betrayed by the routines of life that have been given to you. You feel dead when you no longer feel the need for a future, or when you feel as though the cross that you carry is heavier than what you can possibly hold.

You must believe us when we say that you actually confront death daily in many areas of your life. Simply from the passing of one day to another, you experience a death. That is truly what death feels like when you enter into the spirit world. It feels like the passing of one day to another.

So how do you confront death in peace, not fear? How do you learn to live with the emotion in which death stirs?

First, you must know that experiencing death, a physical death, is as simple as turning the page in a book to read yet another chapter. It feels effortless to the soul making the transition.

Secondly, know that everyday life brings to you a greater welcoming of death in the journey that is ahead of you. Hopefully, by the time you leave the earth you are well prepared for the journey of death that comes, even if you are young of age when death occurs.

Thirdly, you must realize that you are born into life to experience life. Through the experiences of life, you will confront death. That is one of the purposes of living: to close the chapters of your past, and to realize the lessons in which were learned. To learn that death is nothing more than the shifting of your thoughts to a different way with new ideas, new faces, and a new part of you that has been previously hidden from you.

In confronting death, not only physical death, but all deaths, all closures in life, you are humbled when you are able to see death as a blessing, even though it is an event that creates much heartache in your world. But in death there is always a new beginning. If you are able to look past the painful moment of each death, you will see the healing that comes from the ending, the reawakening of yourself, and the beginning of a new life.

It is important to us as your teachers for you to know that if we were to stand in the physical world again, we would have no fear in facing our death. We would embrace our death, for we would know that life in the spirit world is much more peaceful and free than what we would be allowed to live while on earth.

We trust that you know the value of living a physical life. But when you spend so much of your time trying to survive, trying to keep from having death enter into your world too quickly, you scatter the pieces of your life puzzle that were put together for you long before you came into this life. When the pieces of your life puzzle become scattered, nothing in your life makes sense, nothing fits the way that it should. You simply lose interest in living life. You live dead.

Each of you has worked the puzzle of life many times. For that reason, you are well aware of what is healing for you. It is not to have hate in your heart. It is not to hold regrets in your spirit. It is to find a purpose in your life. Finding a purpose is the beginning of putting the pieces of the puzzle back together, of making sense out of your life. For not until you understand the purpose of an event, not until you see and understand the purpose of life as it is being lived, will you ever be able to solve the puzzle of life. It is then that you begin to see that life truly is created so that all the different pieces of you can fit together and bring oneness into that which you call "the closure" – death. Know that everything in your life is a stepping stone to help you confront this last part of your life here on earth.

We ask that you trust us when we say that the longing and pain of those whom we bless always brings pain to our heart, and always brings a need for us to help resurrect the spirit in you that has become worn. From experiencing the heartache of your journey's struggles while on earth, you are sometimes taken back into moments that feel lost, moments in which you feel you confronted death long before your last breath. These painful memories wear on you and take from you your spirit.

It is important to us for you to know that in keeping the memories alive in your heart of those you have lost--the memories of their past, the memories of their spirit--it brings life back to them. It connects these souls to that part of them that once lived. That is why, dear ones, it is so important that you pray for those who have left your world, that you recognize the value of them still in your heart, and that you look at them as a spirit in you that is part of you, and that is not separate from you. Your prayers and love for them allow them to stay alive in their heart with the memories of who they once were and still are in your world. And that, my dear ones, brings to all the peace of life that gives continuation.

Good day.

Chapter 10:
Losses You Must Embrace

When The Guides teach on death, it is always a topic that stirs much interest simply because it does and will affect each and every one of us. Regardless of whom we are or what we do, we will not escape the death tunnel that escorts us into the light. The good news is that on the other side of that tunnel, we meet our families, who will care for us and help us make a smooth transition into our new life. Of course you never leave this earth totally, just as you never leave the spiritual world when you come into life. As long as your soul is alive, which it always is, you will never be alone. How wonderful it is to have that reassurance that there will always be someone to hold your hand when you are afraid, feed you when you are hungry, calm you when you feel pain, and support you while you find your way back into the spirit world.

The Guides speak about death with great warmth, gentleness, and devotion. Maybe it compares to being born here on earth with loving parents and relatives. The only difference is that no soul is ever denied entry back into his real home, God's light.

--Mary Jo

A Teaching from The Guides:

Loss is impossible to escape. It is one of life's obstacles you will most definitely experience at one time or another while living a physical life. There is no degree of loss. All life-changing losses are painful. There are the losses in life that connect you to death, but these are not the only losses of which we speak. We speak of the losses in life that you live and survive more than once in this life.

One of the most devastating losses is the disappointment when souls feel as though their faith is threatened. It is difficult for them to understand "why" when they live committed to the spiritual journey they follow. Their dedication and devotion is tremendous, and yet they suffer such disappointments and hardships when their faith foundation is threatened. They have no energy left in them to continue their devotion after their faith foundation cracks. They feel betrayed and misguided. It is this type of a "living death" that is the most difficult. Others might look at this loss and not be able to understand it, but the pain these souls carry is deep.

In actuality every time a soul suffers loss, it is painful. All sorrow is hurtful, disarming, and demeaning. For the soul experiencing the loss, the pain takes from them their courage, their pride, and sometimes their faith in themselves as well as their Higher Power.

Another difficult loss is the loss of your home, of your foundation in the physical world. With any loss in and of the physical world, the loss of what you value as structure is something that you suffer alone so much of the time. This loss reminds you that you don't always have the support you need. It rips away any sense of security that you might have.

Then there is the loss of your income. You lose what feeds you. You lose the substance to support you and those you love. The loss, the disappointment is so frightening. Without money, you have to depend on someone else to help you survive. This painful loss demands attention in the worst way. It screams that life is changing.

Those who experience loss through death know that the person they have lost cannot be touched again and cannot live again in their reality. They feel there is a part of them that is missing. That part of them hurts and feels empty. Even though their sorrow is intense for the person they lose, their pain can ease somewhat if they have faith that there is a ceremony of silence and peace for the soul in the spiritual realm.

It is most painful for those that mourn the death of the soul that crossed, but it is also sorrowful for the soul who made the transition. They leave behind so much of them. They see the world and yet they are not of the world. Often they feel helpless. This is especially true when they feel the pain from those they love and yet they cannot help heal their pain. Thankfully, their pain is quickly overcome when they are shown that this painful time is short- lived.

So, how do you heal from the losses you experience in life? The first action you need to take is to **embrace your feelings.** The painful emotions will not end suddenly. The way you express and experience your feelings of lost determines the length of time you will mourn.

It is truth that this first action is truly to let go of the wrinkles, the indentations that separate you from the reality of living. When the hard times are there and you feel suffocated with your feelings, confront them, feel them, embrace them, and express them.

The second action is to **live life daily** – moment by moment. Many times you grieve for the continuation of life your loved one lost due to their death. But do not focus on the future. Focus on today. If you overwhelm yourself by the future you dread, the world that is before you, or if you cannot imagine experiencing life without a connection to the one you grieve, it only deepens your pain. Reassure yourself often that they are still part of your world even if you can't sit down with them and have a one-on-one conversation.

The third action is to **be still**. Don't rush to heal. You need to experience the loss. Try to identity the loss in degrees of color. Ask yourself what color your sorrow feels like at this moment. This simple exercise can help you put your arms around your pain. You give your sorrow a name. You make it real.

The fourth action is for when you find yourself missing what you have lost or you are simply wallowing in your pain: **stimulate your life in the world outside of you**. This action helps you to distance yourself from the pain you feel. Work to overcome the pain by helping someone else or looking forward to an upcoming adventure. This simple practice will help you escape the heartache for a short while.

The fifth action is to **strengthen your faith.** Reach into the part of you that hurts. Search for ways that will help you to reconnect to your faith. Faith is hope. Hope is faith. Live today with a hopeful heart. Focus on your grief one day at a time. Live the emotion that is in today.

A good demonstration of this is when parents lose a child. The parents will never overcome their loss completely, but by honoring the memory of their child, they will learn ways to handle their pain. Regardless of how much they would like to turn away from their grief, they know they cannot. They have to embrace their feelings of loss.

It is healing for a parent if they remember their child as they were when they were alive and happy. In truth, they are still alive and happy, for life does not ever end. Life is continuous. Their child is alive and well, living in a different world, in a different reality.

In order for parents to learn about where their child is, we encourage them to read materials on such topics as near-death experiences, books on death and dying, the afterlife, spirituality, and all things that will give them insight and understanding of their child's new world. Also, participating in support groups and studying spiritually deepens their insight, as well.

For those who lose a spouse, it is most difficult for the one left behind. At first, they might find they have so much anger toward the one who left – especially if things are left undone. Often this turns into a much lonelier journey than it should. When this loss occurs, they must force themselves to reach out to those who have walked this journey before them. These souls can offer support and guidance like no one else. They know what it is like when they lose the other half of them.

For those who mourn their parents--and you all will--you need to think of them as being in a peaceful and healing place. Embrace your memories of them. Tell them how grateful you were to have them as your parents. Even though your parents may not have been the parents you wanted them to be, they were the parents you needed them to be. You must always remember that. They created you. Embrace the part of you that grew because of them.

Lastly, take each loss and examine it, embrace it, and feel it. Stop trying to overcome the loss. Experience it. Live your life daily, not weekly, not monthly, and not yearly. Be present with what you feel, not distant from what you feel. Be kind to you, not cross or angry at you. Draw on your strength. If that is your faith, your relationships, they are there as your resource. Draw strength from them. More importantly, feel the pain of what you have lost. It is the only way you will not let it take from you your life.

Good day.

Chapter 11:
When Grief Runs You Over

Meghan's parents tried for so long to survive that they exhausted their resources. Her father's work performance suffered, and her mother failed to care for herself, devoting her emotional resources to the wellbeing of Meghan. After the walls crumbled down on the third anniversary of her death, they experienced the enlightenment that the walk they were on required them to take the next step, which forced them to look inward for peace. For the first time, they looked at what was important to their own grief and allowed themselves to experience it fully.

Over the next year, her parents approached life with a different perspective. They embraced the individual journeys of their friends and family, but were not resistant to openly talk about their own grief. There were no cursory answers. If someone asked, they told them. Most important, they paid attention to their own answers as a sign of their progress. They listened to themselves. They paid attention to the most important person left in their life – them.

Grief and the tragic events of that evening changed their lives forever. It did not change their will for life. It may have altered the course of their journey, but it did not change the end result. They learned that grief was a process, something that is moved through but not overcome. They did not want to forget Meghan, change the image in their mind of her or not feel for her the way they always had. Moving through grief allowed them to live their life while preserving the image of Meghan each and every day. They moved from mourning Meghan to celebrating her life and, most important, their life. That was the way Meghan would have wanted it, and they decided they would not let her down.

Their Loneliest Walk had progressed along the painful journey. What started out as a tragic and devastating event grew to develop both of her parents, individually and as a couple. Her mother and father learned that life had not abandoned them, but that life had forced them to learn more about themselves than at any time before. Grief no longer defined them – it developed them. It was not their identity. They were always Meghan's parents and remain that way today.

The Loneliest Walk – Never Alone – Always with Meghan.

Throughout this book, the process of death, the purpose of change in life, and the emotions of managing and overcoming death have been discussed from a variety of perspectives. It is a natural process, one that should be seen as a graduation instead of a period of mourning. If that is the case, why do you hurt so intensely when a loved one dies or there has been an ending in your life? The change or death is elementary, but the emotional reaction is personal, and that is what makes coping difficult.

There are no standards for managing the pain of grief. Each and every person brings different strengths and challenges to the table. It is a personal walk, a walk that will place great strain on you, much like a long walk that will cause painful blisters on your feet. If you can learn to appreciate that the blisters of your walk are only a temporary discomfort, the overall journey will be rewarding and refreshing. It is all about perspective, and you are in complete control of that.

Grief is not something you overcome; it is something you move through. While the pain may have come on immediately, it does not go away instantaneously. It gets better, and then it gets worse. Something reminds you of your deceased loved one--a smell, a song, an experience--and it triggers many of the emotions you are working hard to move through. The harder you resist, the more intense the emotions are.

If your focus is to overcome grief, each grieving emotion will remind you that your grief is still present, that you have failed at overcoming the challenge before you. The more you remind yourself you have failed to meet your own expectations, the more frustrated you become at your inability to overcome your grief. This is compounded by well-intentioned friends and family members offering their advice and perspectives that your grief should be over by now. How do they know your grieving process? Despite their best intentions, their personal grief walk is theirs, not yours or anyone else's. Their good intentions are setting unreasonable expectations on your own walk, forcing blisters on your feet that normally would not be there. It is like you going on your walk with their shoes on. The shoes do not fit and are sure to hurt your feet. This is how the cycle of grief is maintained and prevents you from moving through grief.

There are three steps critical to understanding how to move through the grieving experience. Everyone has coping skills that can help out, and these three steps are perspectives, not necessarily steadfast rules. Use them on your walk as tools, guides, and supplies.

1. Stop Resisting and Start Experiencing

When the emotions of grief build up, it can be an overwhelming experience. It is unmistakable. The 500-pound elephant moves in to assume its position sitting on your shoulders and chest, placing intense pressure that limits your ability to breath. Your eyes routinely fill with tears, and your head hurts from the pressure. Your friends and family offer to help but do not really know how to help. You fear that if you start talking about it, you will be unable to get it back together. You want to talk about it, but you cannot find anyone who truly understands. The emotional build-up creates pressure beyond your capacity, but even small releases do not sustain. Eventually your emotional gauges move to meltdown mode, and you have a full release of emotions. You lose it.

This scenario is the Grief Tango, and it is played inside the minds of millions of grieving individuals each and every day. It is the sultry dance where you do not get to pick your dance partner. The music is always playing, always just playing in the back of your head.

This cycle continues because you cannot find the appropriate venue to release your emotions. Whether it is guilt, denial, or simply being overwhelmed, you must learn to give yourself the permission to feel what you have been fighting. It is not as bad as you fear. You can keep it together.

When you fight against a natural process, such as your own emotional release, the energy it takes to resist far outweighs the actual thing you fear. Consider all the stories that have been told by lifeguards when you go to the beach. The reason that people drown when taken out by the undertow or current is they exhaust themselves trying to fight against the current. The harder they fight, the worse it gets. Eventually, exhaustion sets in, and they can no longer keep themselves afloat. Kicking, flailing, and trying to survive actually do the opposite. It is panic, simply trying to survive. Sound familiar?

As has been stated in numerous training videos (we are not an official beach training video, mind you) it is best to allow yourself to go with the current. It is more powerful than anything you could ever do. It will eventually bring you back to the shore, in one piece and alive. It takes trust that the process will work, as it has so many times before. When you trust the process and believe you have the ability to overcome any situation in your life, you are more open for help from others, able to find the strength within yourself, and most important, able to draw on your available resources to fight the greatest challenges.

So, how do you go with the current and trust the process?

How do you allow yourself to experience what you fear?

Do you have anything left in your tank? You do, you just might not know it yet.

It is just that, trust. Find time, schedule time for you to be introspective, understanding what emotions you are feeling. Stop resisting. Let it happen. Fifteen minutes a day.

You are the most important person in your life. Regardless of the loss in your life, the feeling that you have lost a part of you, it is important to invest in you. You are no good to anyone else in your world if you are exhausted. Schedule time to experience the emotions you are feeling and fearing.

It is important to understand the purpose of experiencing these emotions. Emotions are reactions to life events. They are very much like a reflex, automatic in response to the world around you. When you "stuff" your emotions, they do not go away. They fester and wait for similar emotions to be stuffed on top of them. When those emotions gain enough support, they finally express themselves -- just not when planned. Emotions that are dealt with or processed do not fester; instead, they are appropriately stored, combined with the memory of the event. This process of storing emotions with memories allows you to remember the good and the bad, to encourage you to do something or give you credence to avoid something. It is a protective mechanism.

Processing of emotions requires introspection. This can be done through any activity that facilitates your review and release of your internal emotions. Therapy, exercise, journaling, meditation, church, or yoga—it does not matter. The activity is personal, part of your walk of moving through grief.

The more time to allocate for you to experience the emotions, to cry, scream, or yell about what you fear or miss since the crossing over, the more it will help reduce the frequency of your emotional meltdowns as well as the intensity. This does not mean you miss them less or no longer hold the personal connection. In fact, quite the opposite. By processing these emotions through planned, scheduled times, you gain greater control and can spend time on more pleasurable experiences.

Fifteen minutes a day, only one percent of the day, scheduled for you. Find a quiet place, an exercise group, a support group. Journal your thoughts and progress. Start out by making you the most important person in your life for fifteen minutes every day.

2. **Birthdays and Anniversary Parties Have Better Gift Bags on The Other Side**

You never stopped loving the individual that crossed over simply because of their death. The calendar did not stop either. Birthdays and anniversaries can be some of the most difficult days of the year when suffering from grief. These important dates can remind you of the truly positive days you had together and the pain you feel now because you are no longer together. They were originally happy days; now, more than likely they are extremely painful. The dates you looked forward to as a child are now dreaded like the first day of school.

It is not uncommon for birthdays and anniversaries to be sources of pain and suffering. What is the appropriate thing to do for their birthday? Do you celebrate it, or do you move on as if it is no longer there? What about other family experiences? Is the family whole if they are not there? How can we have a nice time if they are not here enjoying the family?

One of the most common emotions when these dates come around is guilt and disappointment that family traditions cannot be adhered to as in the past. In fact, many times, the family cautiously avoids conversations or rituals that remind them of their deceased loved one so that they do not have to deal with the painful emotions. Sometimes the unspoken hurts the worst. Start playing the Grief Tango music again.

The fact that your loved one is no longer around does not mean you stop making memories. You cannot stop living your life, so begin incorporating new traditions into these important family activities. At family gatherings, do not avoid traditions or rituals. Instead, take control of your emotions by having time to reflect on things you miss about the loved one, things they enjoyed about that date, a funny story, or simply time to shed a tear or two. This puts you back in control.

By celebrating birthdays, anniversaries and family holidays and incorporating your loved one's memory, it returns these days to a closer image of what they used to be. Most important, it forces you to remember the positive days and openly discuss your thoughts and feelings within your social support. Resist allowing the sharing to take up the day. Have a birthday cake, but don't make it all day. Reflect on your wedding picture album, but do not spend the entire day showing it to loved ones. Allocate the time to be proportional to what you need.

These dates have always been a day to celebrate. It is your responsibility to celebrate and remember their image in the light you desire.

3. Moving Through Grief is a Process – Just Like a Root Canal

Nothing is without a purpose or a plan. Everything impacts you and what you do in life. Grief is no exception. Managing grief has a purpose and follows a process. The process you choose is up to you.

As discussed in the last section, it is important to find the tools to process your own emotions. Whatever the actual activity is does not necessarily matter. The purpose is to learn to find what works for you and when it works. It is part of the process.

There are tremendous support group organizations throughout the country that provide grieving individuals with a safe and supportive environment in which to learn and share their experiences. You can learn from others who are farther down their own walking path. You are not alone. It is time for you to set a strategy and work the process toward your own salvation from the unbearable pain of grief.

Regardless of the actual comprehensive program you choose to follow, it is important to maintain a healthy perspective of the process. The Grief Tango music is always playing in the background, so falling into the cycle of setting yourself up for unrealistic expectations and getting frustrated by your progress will only sabotage your developmental walk. It is a challenge to maintain a healthy perspective and focus. Choose a plan and walk it with reasonable expectations.

There are no timelines for grief. It is truly personal. Clinically speaking, grief and depression can look a lot alike, and grief can absolutely lead to depression. If you feel your grief has persisted and significantly impacted your ability to function in life, work, or with your family, please seek professional help. Death of a loved one is a significant stress in life. It can greatly impact anyone's functioning.

However, grief can also be managed before it progresses to full-blown, clinical depression.

The walk you are on can seem like you are about to climb Mount Everest. It can be daunting and overwhelming. The truth, your ideal goal for your mental health, does not lie at the top of Mount Everest. Instead, the truth you desire lies right in front of your next step. We have advocated for several years that individuals suffering from grief apply The One Percent Principle as a way to manage expectations and learn to see that the progress you desire is right in front of you.

The One Percent Principle asserts that growth and change, from any situation, is a process based on a series of small changes, improvements, and building blocks. Together and in succession, they create great growth and sustained change. The mistake many make is their focus is always on where they want to go, the endpoint, instead of on the process.

This perspective is the Grief Tango in real life. When faced with any challenge or opportunity, understanding that change occurs in one-percent increments is the next step on your walk. Focus on seeing your grief improvement one percent at a time. One step, one day, one percent at a time.

It is a perspective – your perspective.

Ask yourself the following:

> Can today be just one percent better than yesterday?

> Can I give myself the opportunity to spend one percent of my day, fifteen minutes, on myself, whether it is to be emotional or not have to worry about my grief?

> Am I in control of things that make me sad in my life? If not, then is it worth my time worrying about it?

> If each day I improved one percent, would I be better off in one week?

The One Percent Principle is based on the principle of compound interest. The efforts you must expend to improve can be overwhelming, but trust that the one percent improvements will lead to greater change DOWN THE WALK. Each day is an improvement. Since you only want to improve by one percent, it really does not take a whole lot of your own resources or effort to make the small differences.

As The One Percent Principle accompanies you on your walk, use realistic outcomes to see if you have had progress. Journal your activities, monitor your crying sessions and evaluate if you are able to do more in your life. Any improvement, no matter how big or small, is an IMPROVEMENT. Each gradual improvement sets the stage for the next one.

Experience life the way you want to live life. It is a journey, not a destination. Each day, one percent better. Allow yourself to laugh, to cry and to be angry. Search for answers in the world, and search for answers within you. Seek to communicate with your loved one, whether simply by talking to them, dreaming about them, or laughing at things they used to laugh at.

Find a support group, a church group or a reading team to study and learn. Life is about learning. The hardest lessons have the greatest rewards. Help someone else who is grieving by listening and serving as an example. You may not know who needs that support. Listen to the people in your life, from close family to complete strangers. They have a story to tell and a life to impact.

Join an association that keeps your loved one's image alive. Plant a tree, take a memory walk. Celebrate their birthday, anniversary, and special occasions. They did not stop being a part of you simply because they crossed over. Your love did not end. It continues. Continue to celebrate it.

Allow yourself the opportunity to grieve, to learn about who you are and what you need out of life. The next person you meet may need you more than you need them. Open your heart and you will change the world. There is no question the death of your loved one or the ending of an aspect of your life is a living tragedy. If you could reverse time, you would reverse the outcome. Unfortunately, you cannot change the course of history. The only thing you can change is how you live forward. That is up to you.

You started your own loneliest walk when your loved one crossed over. The question was not whether you were going to start the walk. The question was how. You never lost sight of where you wanted to go; you simply lost focus on how you were going to get there. The walk starts with the next step, the true one percent.

The Loneliest Walk – Do Not Go It Alone.

Appendix A:
Tips for Finding a Valuable Support Group

The following is a list of suggestions for finding a support group or organization that is right for you.

1. Do not stop looking until you find the right support group for you. Ask friends, family, doctors, and pastors which support groups they recommend. It is important that you find a group that challenges you, makes you think about the feelings you are experiencing, and makes you work at getting better. Support groups are not simply to share your story, they are for you to get better and improve.

2. Don't get frustrated if the first meeting or group does not meet up to your expectations. Attend the next meeting or find a different group that may be made up of different individuals. Support groups are beneficial because of the involvement of the members.

3. Listen to the other members. You may want to share your story in the beginning, but there is time for that. Listen to others in the group because they may have something to offer.

4. Be honest with your feelings and concerns. You cannot learn from the others in the group unless you are honest with yourself.

5. Finally, go. Don't find excuses not to attend. Find the reasons why it is important that you do attend. Remember, you are the most important person in your life. Treat yourself that way.

Biography - Mary Jo McCabe

Since 1981, Mary Jo McCabe has touched the lives of individuals looking for greater understanding and guidance to many of life's greatest challenges. From managing the pain of grief to understanding each person's soul purpose, Mary Jo defies the traditional stereotypes to offer hope, insight, and direction in a variety of settings and venues. Do not call her a psychic, even though she hosts a popular radio program – *The Psychic and The Doc Radio Program* – by that title. Do not call her a medium, she reserves that for her medium colleagues like John Edward. What should you call Mary Jo McCabe? Simply the best.

Through her organization, The McCabe Institute and her live call-in, syndicated radio show with her son, Dr. Bhrett McCabe - *The Psychic and The Doc Radio Program*, Mary Jo offers a distinctive lifeline for individuals and families when the traditional approaches simply fall short. Whether through private consultations, group sessions, or media appearances, Mary Jo McCabe brings her professional, modern approach that is honest and refreshing to clients, associates, and the media alike. Working with a group she affectionately refers to as The Guides, Mary Jo delivers their message with an amazing accuracy that often leaves individuals wanting more.

An accomplished author, Mary Jo has written several books, including *Learn to See: An Approach to Your Inner Voice Through Symbols*, *Come This Way: A Better Life Awaits*, *It All Begins Here: Interpreting Your Dreams*, and *Cracking the Coconut Code: 7 Insights to Transform Your Life*, which was published by John Edward's Princess Books in December 2004. She recently released *Transforming Life Into Living* with her son, Dr. Bhrett McCabe, a workbook designed to stop letting life live you and start living the life you desire. Mary Jo has also worked with leaders in the field of self-empowerment, including psychic medium, John Edward, who provided his recommendation in his best-selling book, *One Last Time*, as well as an invited contributor to his online resource - Infinite Quest, providing teachings and commentary for individuals seeking greater self-fulfillment.

Mary Jo lives with her husband, Jim, in Niceville, Florida. She enjoys spending time with her son, Bhrett, his wife, Melissa, and their two children, Logan and Caroline.

Biography - Dr. Bhrett McCabe

Dr. Bhrett McCabe has the innate ability to empower people to reach their full potential. Committed to individual fulfillment, Dr. McCabe has effectively merged learnings from his own upbringing with the traditional academic lessons throughout his professional development. Through lectures, appearances, and personal consultations, Dr. McCabe's approach emphasizes the individual abilities within each of us to achieve those personal and professional aspirations that lie within everyone.

A licensed clinical psychologist, Dr. McCabe earned his Ph.D. in Clinical Psychology from Louisiana State University, with an emphasis in Behavioral Medicine/Health Psychology, and an internship with the Clinical Psychology Training Consortium at the Brown University School of Medicine. Dr. McCabe's clinical/research training and academic publications have involved understanding how general psychological principles impact the coping, management, and disease course of general medical conditions.

A four year letterman on the Louisiana State University baseball team (1991-1995) and a member of two NCAA Championship teams (1991 & 1993), three Southeastern Conference regular season championship teams (1991-1993), and three College World Series teams (1991, 1993, & 1994), Dr. McCabe has developed a respected practice with professional and amateur athletes by applying his on-field experiences with his understanding of complex principles underlying athletic, professional, and personal success. As a result of these consultations, Dr. McCabe developed The One Percent Principle highlighting the role that small, incremental changes have on managing change and achieving success.

Very active in the community, Dr. McCabe has played an integral role in several large fundraisers for a variety of causes throughout the Southeast U.S. Dr. McCabe lives with his wife, Melissa and their two daughters, Logan and Caroline, in Birmingham, AL.

CPSIA information can be obtained at www.ICGtesting.com
Printed in the USA
242481LV00003B/165/P